Lambi Learns About Addiction
A Book About Prevention

Written by Trish Luna
Written by Kellie Montana

For my children and grandchildren who have my heart —
Nick, Sami, Maddie, Vivien, Nico, and Owen.

Printed and bound in the United States of America.
10987654321
Revised Edition

Library of Congress Cataloging-in-Publication data is on file with the publisher.

According to the National Association for Children of Addiction (NACoA), one out of every four kids in America is growing up in a family adversely impacted by addiction to drugs or alcohol. Children are the first hurt and last helped. Addiction is a disease of isolation, silence, secrecy, shame, and stigma. Living in an environment of chaos, inconsistency, and unpredictability, many believe it's all their fault. They may feel confused, scared, sad, hurt, and guilty. Despite all these inherent risks, they are children of promise.

"Lambi Learns about Addiction: A Book about Prevention" is an excellent resource to help these children. Lambi helps kids understand about the disease of addiction and how it is not their fault. It offers a variety of coping skills, such as the ability to identify and express feelings in healthy ways, mindful breathing, and the importance of play and fun. This gem especially helps youngsters to realize that they are not alone.

When a family member, other caregiver, or a professional reads with a child about Lambi's journey, it not only allows a true connection to build, but also offers the opportunity to talk about a difficult problem in a caring, nurturing way. I can't think of any kid I've worked with through the years who wouldn't deeply benefit from the powerful messages in Lambi's story. It will undoubtedly put that child on a healing path.

Jerry Moe, MA
National Director of Children's Programs (retired)
Hazelden Betty Ford Foundation

My name is Lambi ... but I am a *bunny!*
Isn't that strange and isn't that funny?
You'd think I'd be a lamb, but I have long ears,
You'll see not everything is as it appears.
I'll show you more things that are not what you think,
Like how people can change after too much to drink.

Have you heard of addiction? A **HARD** word to say,
It's a disease, and it hurts families each day.
It can hurt a mom, brother, sister or dad,
But, trust me, it's **NOT** something
they wish they had.

When someone gets sick with a cold, flu, or cancer,
Everyone tries to come up with an answer.

But addiction is met with shame and with blame,
Diseases are not always treated the same.
This makes my heart hurt, and I feel PAIN inside,
I don't want to see friends. I just want to hide.
I worry and wonder: *Did I cause this mess?*
It makes me feel sad — and I feel lots of stress.

Addiction's a problem you can't always SEE,
And that is how it is with MOMMY and ME.

Her addiction is bad ... a really big deal!
Sometimes she does things that just don't seem real.

Things start to change from
being happy and calm,
To feeling unsafe — I
don't recognize Mom.

Sometimes my fears grow so big in my head ...
Like a **GIANT** balloon — all BIG, bright and red.
When feelings get stuck, like they're here to stay,
I've learned a cool trick that helps move them away.

I let go of the string — you might wonder *why*?
I've learned feelings move fast, and I let them FLY!
Now this doesn't mean that the problem is gone,
But this DOES help my brain to find peace and feel calm.

I also imagine I'm holding my *heart*,
I hold it so close, so it won't break apart!
I have some good friends who know just how I feel,
And safe, trusted people can help me to heal.

They tell me Mom's problems are not caused by me
I'm so happy to hear that — *don't you agree?*
Hearing and learning that I'm not to blame,
Makes me feel better and helps lift my shame.

There are other things that I've learned about, too,
Like my body speaks to me — yours speaks to you!
I've learned to listen to hear what it says,
Sometimes it's my tummy. Sometimes it's my head!
The pain in my tummy is one way to say,
"*I'm not quite alright,*" and, "*I'm not quite OK.*"
Sometimes it's my head ... like a big block of wood,
it says, "*Nothing feels nice,*" and, "*Nothing feels good.*"

When I sit on the ground, it makes me feel still,
It might work for you ... and I sure hope it will.
I take some DEEP breaths ... I breathe IN, I breathe OUT,
feeling ROOTED and GROUNDED is what it's about!

Once I feel GROUNDED, I let my mind go ...
I see beaches ... and mountains all covered in snow.
Imagining places is fun — you can try it!
Remember ... it's good to feel calm and find quiet.

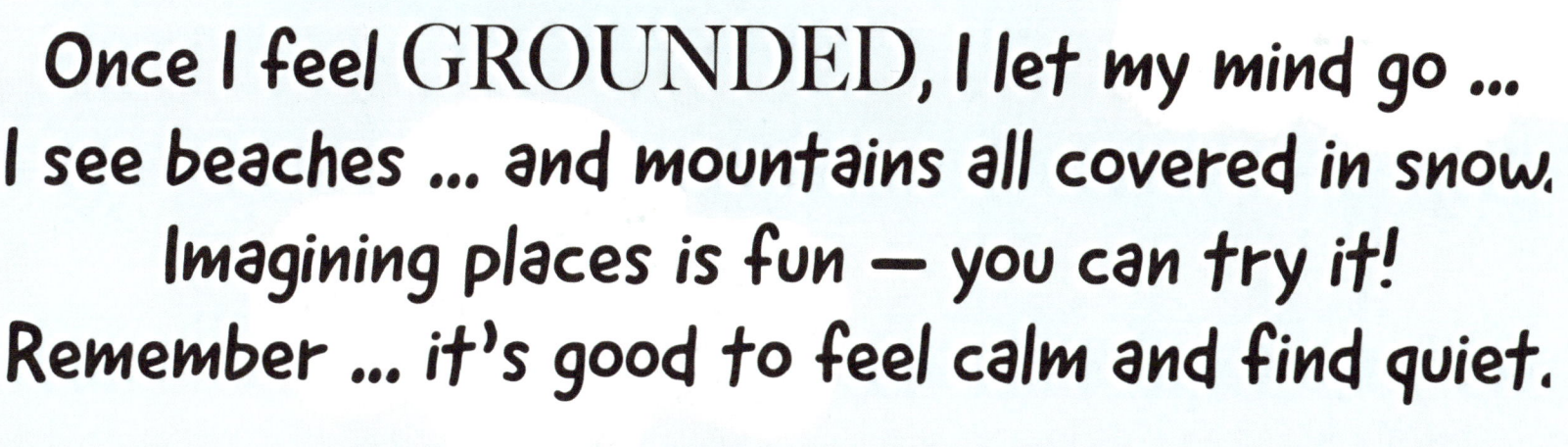

Hugging my pillow, or singing a song,
Makes me feel **HAPPY** and makes me feel **STRONG**.
I flap like a bird! Twirl my ears all around,
Tapping my sides helps my body calm down.
Brushing off worries — get them off with a sweep,
That helps me let go when my feelings are deep.

I go find a friend and play catch with a ball,
Or just go outside — that's the BEST thing of all!
Being in nature makes my insides feel right,
My head feels more calm, and my tummy less tight.

Now ... as I grow up, I'll have CHOICES to make,
Which road to go down, and which path to TAKE.
As I think of the future, and I look ahead,
I think what my safe, trusted people have said:
"Be careful what choices you make when you choose,
The choices decide if you win — or you lose."

Trouble

Safety

It might look like fun, and it might seem real cool,
When you see some kids breaking rules at your school.
But take it from Lambi — it's NOT a good choice.
Just stop… and Listen to your **STRONG** inner voice.
"That's not a good choice," says the voice in your head,
"I am true to my heart — I want good things instead."

So, join your friend Lambi and say a loud "No!"
You have good things to do — good places to go!

I want to live healthy! I know what drugs do,
I'll stay away from them — I hope you do, too!

Be true to your heart and choose the best thing,
Go find some good friends and
go run, play, and sing!

So now that my story is just about done,
I hope you LEARNED something, but also had **FUN.**
There are things you *can't* change, and you *can't* control,
To feel **GROUNDED** but lighter — that is the goal!
Move your feelings along ... you might feel better,
Things you can do alone — some all together.

Remember that Lambi will always be here,
I'll always listen with my very **BIG** ears!
I have the same feelings that you have ... it's true,
I'm sending my **LOVE** — right from Lambi to YOU!

I hope this book can help you help the child in your life who needs language, validation, and coping skills to deal with the fallout from the substance abuse of a loved one. This has been my family's story.

"What is mentionable is manageable." — Fred Rogers

Substance use disorder (SUD) affects millions of families, including mine. My goal is to create a safe space for open and compassionate conversations, supporting the whole family. It is most helpful when we offer assistance and support rather than judgment, criticism, and blame. Read the book at the child's pace, respecting their comfort. Stay calm, have fun, maybe make up a song or do something playful. Encourage emotional release and self-compassion — give yourself a hug!

Thank you for sharing this story and for being a safe, trusted person for a child who needs you,

Trish

Thank you to my children, Nicholas, and Samantha, for walking this journey with me. We lost their father, Joe, to this disease. He left a hole in our hearts and an indelible mark on our lives. To my husband, Pat, for loving, supporting, and believing in me. To my granddaughters, Maddie, and Vivien, who live on the front line of this disease and were brave enough to share their story. To my mother, Madeline, for being our safe place to land when we needed it. She was the gravity that held us in place. To my sister, Janet, for her invaluable contribution and insights into the importance of including approachable mindfulness and other evidence-based practices when helping traumatized children to heal. I could not have done it without her. To my dear friend, Kellie, who is the sole reason this story came to life — thanks to her tender heart, her incredible gifts as an artist, her attention to the tiniest detail, her humor, and her steadfast commitment — not only to our friendship, but to the millions of kids who need to "see" themselves in a book.

A deep and special thanks to all the people I am blessed to have in my life who "saw" that this was a necessary story. Tabatha, Stacee, Eric, Jerry, Shandi, Micki, Lori, Janel, Greg, Beth, Lisa, Jamie, Dan, Derek, Tim, Beth & Dave, Virginia, Sandy & Ellen, Deb & Keith, Allen, Terry, Brian, Brandon, Sissy, and Matt, Marielena, Rusty, along with many others on the front lines of combating childhood trauma.

Nashville, Tennessee-based author, speaker, trainer Trish Luna has a master's degree in philosophy and ethics from Vanderbilt University and has a diverse professional background. "Lambi" continues her life's work. She is an in-demand speaker and trainer of Lambi Learns (TM) Academy in schools, police departments, community coalitions, court programs, treatment centers, nonprofits, and professional conferences.
Please visit: www.lambilearns.com
Contact: Info@lambilearns.com